THE SYSTEM™ 6X6 FRAMEWORK

The Ultimate Guide to Performance, Resilience, and Cycling Mastery

I0559635

by

David Lipscomb

THE SYSTEM™ 6X6 FRAMEWORK

Copyrights © 2025 David Lipscomb

All rights reserved.

Case ID: 1-14896185211

LCCN: 2025906223

Paperback ISBN: 978-1-967178-45-2

Acknowledgments

This book would not have been possible without the dedication, support, and inspiration of many individuals who have contributed to developing THE SYSTEM™ 6x6 Framework.

First and foremost, I would like to express my deepest gratitude to my athletes—those who have trusted in this methodology, put in the work, and demonstrated the power of structured training. Your progress and success continue to be the greatest validation of this system.

Thank you to my coaching mentors and peers for your insights, feedback, and continuous motivation to refine and improve this framework. Your wisdom and expertise have played a crucial role in shaping THE SYSTEM™ into what it is today.

To my family and close friends, your unwavering support, encouragement, and belief in this vision have provided the foundation for this work. Your patience through the long hours of research, training, and coaching means the world to me.

Special thanks to the cycling and endurance sports community for fostering an environment of continuous learning, pushing boundaries, and sharing knowledge that has helped evolve this methodology.

Finally, to all readers, athletes, and coaches embarking on this journey with THE SYSTEM™, I appreciate your commitment to growth and excellence. May this book serve as a guiding tool to unlock your full potential and achieve sustainable success.

Thank you all.

Disclaimer

The information presented in this book is for educational and informational purposes only. The recommendations and training methodologies outlined are based on extensive coaching experience, scientific research, and data analysis but should not be interpreted as medical or professional healthcare advice.

Readers should consult with a physician or qualified healthcare provider before starting any new exercise program, particularly if they have pre-existing medical conditions or concerns. The author and publisher disclaim any liability for injury, loss, or damages resulting from the use or application of the strategies and principles discussed in this book.

Individual results may vary, and no guarantees of performance improvements or specific outcomes are made. Success depends on multiple factors, including an athlete's dedication, consistency, and adherence to proper training principles.

Contents

About This Book

THE SYSTEM™ 6x6 Framework is more than just a training method—it's a revolutionary approach that combines science, structure, and strategy to maximize athletic performance. Rooted in decades of coaching experience and performance data analysis, this book explores the six core pillars of THE SYSTEM™, providing athletes and coaches with a comprehensive roadmap to success.

From energy system mastery and endurance training to mental resilience and leadership, this guide breaks down the key elements required for sustained peak performance. Whether you are a competitive cyclist, an endurance athlete, or a coach looking to refine your methods, THE SYSTEM™ provides a proven, repeatable framework to unlock your full potential.

What You'll Learn:

- **How to optimize all six energy systems** for endurance, power, and performance gains.

- **Structured training strategies** that balance volume, intensity, and recovery.

- **The psychology of high-performance athletes** and how to develop resilience.

- **Advanced periodization techniques** to peak at the right time.

- **Case studies from elite athletes** who have implemented THE SYSTEM™ successfully.

- **How to avoid common training mistakes** and maximize long-term progression.

Prepare to revolutionize your training, sharpen your mental game, and take your performance to levels you never thought possible. This is THE SYSTEM™—your blueprint for success.

About Coach David and THE SYSTEM™

Coach David has spent over 30 years in endurance sports, blending his extensive experience as an athlete, coach, and innovator. His coaching philosophy is deeply rooted in data-driven performance metrics, structured progression, and a holistic approach to athlete development. Drawing inspiration from martial arts, neuroscience, and sports science, he has developed a methodology integrating physical and mental conditioning to optimize performance. His passion lies in empowering athletes to push beyond their limits and achieve breakthroughs in endurance and power-based disciplines.

About THE SYSTEM™

THE SYSTEM™ is more than a training plan—it is a comprehensive **6x6 Framework** designed to develop every aspect of an athlete's performance. Built on six core components—training Elements, Energy Systems, Performance Standards, Core Philosophies, Emotional Intelligence Skills, and Leadership Elements—THE SYSTEM™ provides a structured, repeatable, and scientifically backed method to help athletes reach and sustain peak performance. Whether you're an elite competitor or an amateur seeking consistent improvement, THE SYSTEM™ offers a roadmap to unlocking true potential.

Why This Matters:

In the words of David Lipscomb:

"Mastery isn't an accident—it's engineered. THE SYSTEM™ 6x6 Framework is more than a methodology; it's a blueprint for sustainable performance, built on precision, balance, and execution. Whether you're an elite competitor or an ambitious athlete, this system will redefine the way you train, think, and perform."

— **David Lipscomb**

This commitment to ***precision, balance, and adaptability*** is what sets THE SYSTEM™ apart, making it a game-changer for athletes who are serious about maximizing their potential.

Preface

The System™ 6x6 Manifesto: Redefining Cycling Performance

What This Manifesto Represents

The System™ 6x6 Manifesto is more than a document—it's a declaration of purpose, a blueprint for transformation, and a commitment to sustainable performance. It embodies the principles of structured mastery, continuous refinement, and data-driven coaching that define CIS Training Systems.

This manifesto is for:

- The beginner seeking clarity in their training journey.

- The competitive cyclist striving to break through plateaus and reach new heights.

- The lifelong athlete dedicated to continuous improvement and long-term success.

It is a reminder that cycling performance isn't about short-term gains or random workouts. It's about strategy, execution, and mastering every element that contributes to peak performance.

The Problem: Why Traditional Training Fails Cyclists

For decades, cyclists have followed the same outdated approach:

- Training plans based on arbitrary FTP numbers.

- Intervals that leave riders burned out instead of stronger.

- A focus on peak power without endurance to sustain it.

- A lack of structured mastery—just random sessions that don't build long-term success.

This system has failed athletes at every level. Riders who should be thriving are stuck in plateaus, burnout, and frustration. They train hard but never truly break through. They are told that power is everything, yet they cannot sustain their power when it matters.

The real problem? Cyclists aren't training with a system.

The truth is, sustainable cycling performance isn't about training harder—it's about training smarter, systematically, and progressively.

This is why I created The System™ 6x6—a proven methodology that integrates endurance, power, energy system development, and performance intelligence into a structured progression that delivers measurable results, real mastery, and sustainable success.

The Birth of The System™ 6x6: A New Approach to Performance

I didn't just create The System™ in theory—I built it from three decades of experience in performance coaching, martial arts mastery, elite cycling competition, corporate change management, and continuous improvement methodologies like Six Sigma.

I started building this model in April 2006, after years of seeing cyclists train hard without results. I knew there had to be a better way—one that wasn't based on guesswork or outdated traditions, but on structured progression, mastery, and real-world application. Through my experience coaching athletes across disciplines and my background in Human Resources and Whole Systems Transformation, I identified patterns of success that transcended sport and business:

- Sustainable endurance and power aren't achieved by isolated workouts but by a system of interconnected training principles.

- Mastery isn't about working harder—it's about working smarter, refining technique, and focusing on precision.

- Every successful athlete follows a structured path—whether in martial arts, cycling, or elite competition.

- Change must be holistic—every component of an athlete's performance affects the whole system, just as in business transformation.

The Martial Arts, Six Sigma & Change Management Connection: Mastery Over Metrics

Before I was a cycling coach, I was a martial artist, trained in Cuong Nhu Oriental Martial Arts and achieved Black Belt Status in 1993. Martial arts taught me a fundamental truth: progress isn't random. You don't just fight harder—you train systematically, refining your technique, developing neuromuscular control, and progressing toward mastery.

- Every movement matters.

- Every drill builds precision and efficiency.

- Progression is earned—not given.

Similarly, Six Sigma principles focus on eliminating inefficiencies and refining execution for optimal results. In the business world, Six Sigma revolutionized how organizations operate by focusing on precision, repeatability, and continuous improvement—principles that directly apply to athletic performance.

Additionally, my experience in corporate Human Resources and Whole Systems Transformation reinforced the importance of system-wide change. Whole Systems Transformation is an approach that enables organizations to accomplish faster, cheaper, and sustainable positive change. The Systems Approach of Change Management teaches that change must be holistic in nature, taking into consideration all interrelated variables and how they influence each other.

- Changing one component of a system affects the entire system, whether in business or athletic performance.

- A structured approach to change enables athletes to adapt faster and achieve sustained growth.

- Transformation isn't just about improving one metric—it's about optimizing the entire system for peak performance.

When I transitioned into coaching cyclists, I saw the same principles of mastery and continuous improvement missing from endurance training. Cyclists were training hard but not training with precision. Their workouts lacked intent, balance, and structured development. Most followed cookie-cutter training plans that didn't account for energy system balance, progressive overload, or long-term performance sustainability.

Just as a martial artist advance from White Belt to Black Belt through disciplined training and structured mastery, cyclists should advance through a progressive system that develops their energy systems, technical skills, and strategic execution over time.

This is why The System™ 6x6 was built—to bring together structured training, real-world application, and performance mastery in a way that had never been done before.

The System™ 6x6 is built on these principles:

- **Precision Training:** Every ride, every session has a purpose—random rides don't build sustainable performance.

- **Mastery Through Progression:** Athletes must develop step by step, just like earning belts in martial arts.

- **Data-Driven Execution:** Success is measurable. Training must be structured and evaluated based on real performance metrics, not guesswork.

- **Continuous Refinement:** Training isn't static—it evolves with the athlete, ensuring sustained growth without burnout.

- **Systems-Based Approach:** Just as in business transformation, peak performance requires managing all interconnected variables for optimal efficiency.

The System™ 6x6: The Framework for Cycling Mastery

Instead of focusing on one or two training components, The System™ optimizes ALL aspects of cycling performance through a structured, progressive model. To ensure complete mastery in cycling performance, The System™ 6x6 follows a structured matrix that integrates training elements, energy systems, prime level standards, core philosophies, EQ-i® skills, and leadership traits:

The 6 Training Elements: What You Must Master

- **Endurance Training** – The foundation of all cycling success. Without endurance, nothing else matters.

- **Cadence Control** – The ability to generate power efficiently across all terrains and situations.

- **Force/Tempo Development** – Strength training on the bike that builds durability and resilience.

- **Speed Endurance** – The ability to maintain high speed over sustained efforts.

- **Power Generation** – Explosive efforts for critical attacks, surges, and sprint finishes.

- **Threshold/Lactate Clearance** – The key to pushing beyond limits without fatigue setting in.

The 6 Energy Systems You Must Develop

- **Pmax (Peak Power Output)** – Your explosive power in surges and sprints.

- **VO2 Max** – The ability to sustain high-intensity work.

- **TTE (Time to Exhaustion)** – How long you can hold your threshold power.

- **FRC (Functional Reserve Capacity)** – Your anaerobic power reserve.

- **MFTP (Maximal Functional Threshold Power)** – Your true measure of sustainable power.

- **Stamina** – The ability to ride strong for hours without fading.

The 6 Prime Level Standards: Elevating Your Athletic Performance

- **Focus, Mental Resilience** – Strengthen your mental endurance under stress.

- **Confidence** – Build self-belief in your technical ability.

- **Drive** – Cultivate intrinsic motivation to push beyond limits.

- **Confidence, Focus** – Stay engaged under race conditions.

- **Intensity** – Maintain high effort over key moments.

- **Emotion** – Channel emotions effectively in training.

The 6 Core Philosophies: Guiding Your Training & Execution

- **Adaptability & Resilience** – Maintain performance in changing conditions.

- **Effort Control & Execution** – Execute pacing strategies with precision.

- **Discipline & Consistency** – Establish structured and repeatable habits.

- **Energy System Mastery** – Optimize training loads for sustained progress.

- **Continuous Learning & Growth** – Develop strategies for long-term success.

- **Balance & Recovery** – Ensure longevity in your training progress.

The 6 EQ-i® Skills: Mastering Your Mental & Emotional Game

- **Stress Tolerance** – Strengthen your ability to remain calm under pressure.

- **Self-Regard** – Recognize and leverage your strengths and weaknesses.

- **Impulse Control** – Manage energy output effectively for sustained efforts.

- **Emotional Awareness** – Understand how emotions impact your performance.

- **Self-Actualization** – Strive for continuous personal improvement.

- **Independence** – Make informed decisions without over-reliance on external guidance.

The 6 Leadership Traits: Becoming a Stronger Athlete & Competitor

- **Accountability** – Take full responsibility for your training and progress.

- **Communication** – Effectively convey strategy and feedback to improve results.

- **Vision** – Set long-term goals and develop a strategic training pathway.

- **Influence** – Lead by example to inspire others in the sport.

- **Resilience** – Recover quickly from setbacks and maintain composure.

- **Adaptability** – Adjust dynamically to race conditions and training challenges.

Training Elements	Energy Systems	Prime Level Standards	Core Philosophies	EQ-i® Skills	Leadership
Endurance Training Develops aerobic capacity for sustained performance	**Stamina, MFTP** Supports long-duration efforts with efficiency.	**Focus, Mental Resilience** Enhances mental endurance under stress.	**Adaptability & Resilience** Maintains performance in changing conditions.	**Stress Tolerance** Ability to remain calm under pressure.	**Accountability** Commitment to consistent effort and improvement.
Cadence Control Optimizes pedaling efficiency and power output.	**Neuromuscular** Enhances coordination and smooth execution.	**Confidence** Builds self-belief in technical ability.	**Effort Control & Execution** Maintains precision in pacing strategies	**Self-Regard** Recognizing one's strengths and weaknesses.	**Communication** Effectively conveying strategy and feedback.
Force/Tempo Development Builds muscular endurance for sustained power.	**FRC, TTE** Improves resistance to fatigue over time.	**Drive** Intrinsic motivation to push beyond limits.	**Discipline & Consistency** Establishes structured and repeatable habits.	**Impulse Control** Managing energy output effectively	**Vision** Setting long-term goals and training pathways.
Speed Endurance Maintains high velocity over long distances.	**VO2 Max** Increases oxygen efficiency for high intensities.	**Confidence, Focus** Staying engaged under race conditions.	**Energy System Mastery** Understanding how to optimize training loads.	**Emotional Awareness** Understanding how emotions impact performance.	**Influence** Leading by example to inspire others.
Power Generation Boosts peak output for sprints and surges.	**Pmax, FRC** Enhances short-burst power capacity.	**Intensity** Maintaining high effort over key moments.	**Continuous Learning & Growth** Developing strategies for long-term gains.	**Self-Actualization** Striving for personal improvement.	**Resilience** Recovering quickly from setbacks.
Threshold/Lactate Clearance Increases ability to clear and utilize lactate.	**MFTP, Recovery** Extends time at sustainable power output.	**Emotion** Channeling emotions effectively in training.	**Balance & Recovery** Ensuring longevity in training progress.	**Independence** Making informed decisions without reliance	**Adaptability** Adjusting to race conditions dynamically.

The CIS Community: A Movement Rooted in 170+ Years of Collective Experience

The System™ is more than a training methodology—it's a movement. It represents the collective wisdom, passion, and dedication of a global network of cyclists and coaches who believe in training smarter, not just harder.

With over 170 years of active membership, and growing, the CIS Training Systems community has pushed the boundaries of endurance sports, evolving through data-driven insights, real-world applications, and shared knowledge. This is a community of high-performance athletes, weekend warriors, and competitive racers, all united by a common pursuit: mastery of the sport.

- **Real riders. Real experience. Real progress.** Every athlete contributes to the ecosystem, offering lessons, challenges, and breakthroughs that push the group forward.

- **A culture of continuous improvement.** We don't just train—we refine, adapt, and evolve. Every ride, every effort is a step toward personal and collective excellence.

- **More than numbers—it's about mastery.** Training metrics are valuable, but true performance is built on discipline, execution, and the relentless pursuit of progress.

- **A legacy of elite coaching.** The CIS community thrives on mentorship, shared wisdom, and the belief that knowledge grows stronger when passed on.

This is not just a training program—it's a collective force, a legacy of performance-driven athletes committed to reaching new heights. When you train with The System™, you don't train alone. You become part of a movement that is rewriting what's possible in endurance training.

The Philosophy Behind The System™: Coaching vs. Training

Most cyclists follow training plans—but training alone isn't enough. Coaching is about developing an athlete holistically, ensuring their mentality, execution, and physiological systems all align for success.

Martial Arts Philosophy in Cycling Coaching: You don't just "train"—you refine, adapt, and master skills over time. Every ride has a purpose—random rides don't build sustainable performance. Training progression must be structured—just like earning belts in martial arts. That's why The System™ has a MasterClass progression, with athletes working towards higher-level mastery (Green Belt, Brown Belt, Black Belt, and beyond).

The Black Belt MasterClass Program: A Path to True Cycling Mastery

Unlike traditional coaching, The System™ follows a structured progression, much like a martial arts belt system.

Every athlete starts at White Belt, learning the fundamentals of endurance and power development. As they train, progress, and refine their skills, they advance through the ranks, eventually reaching Black Belt status—a true master of The System™.

The Mastery Levels of The System™

- **White Belt (Foundation Phase)** – Learning the basics of heart rate and its impact on endurance, and cadence control.

- **Yellow Belt (Structured Progression)** – Developing aerobic efficiency and fatigue resistance.

- **Green Belt (Intermediate Mastery)** – Building sustainable power, speed endurance, and knowledge transfer.

- **Brown Belt (Advanced Development)** – Fine-tuning race execution, neuromuscular efficiency, and high-performance metrics.

- **Black Belt (Elite Mastery & Coaching Readiness)** – Reaching full mastery of The System™, unlocking race-winning power, and qualifying to mentor others.

Real-World Proof: How The System™ Transformed Performance

- **Scottie Weiss – 2016 UCI Masters World Champion** Using The System™'s HR and Power-Based Workouts, Scottie optimized his endurance and neuromuscular efficiency, leading to a UCI World Championship win in Time Trial and Road.

- **Santiago Pelaez – Category 1 Racer Transformation**
Santiago came in strong but lacked sustainable endurance. By training Cadence Control, Speed Endurance, VO2 Max and Force Development together, he completely redefined his racing performance in just 97 days resulting in multiple podium finishes.

- **Lance Smith – Unlocking Sustainable Power** Lance was a high-intensity club rider but struggled with fatigue in long group rides. By restructuring his training with Breaking Through Plateaus by optimizing Endurance & Lactate Clearance to turn long rides into power-dominant performances.

Why The System™ Matters for Cyclists at Every Level

No matter your starting point—whether you're new to cycling and aiming for efficiency or an elite racer seeking the next breakthrough—**The System™ 6x6** is built to elevate your performance:

- **Data-Driven, Experience-Backed:** It merges advanced cycling metrics with real-world coaching expertise, ensuring your training isn't just theoretical but practical and results-driven.

- **Customized to Your Strengths:** Whether you excel as a sprinter, climber, or endurance rider, The System™ refines your strengths while systematically addressing weaknesses, making you a more complete athlete.

- **Prevents Burnout & Stagnation:** By balancing all six training elements, it ensures structured progression, avoiding overtraining while optimizing adaptation and recovery for long-term success.

The Future: Elevating The System™ for 2025 & Beyond

With The System™ evolving into Breakthrough Coaching, MasterClass programs, and educational summits and retreats, the goal is simple:

- Redefine what's possible in endurance training.

- Make elite-level performance accessible to more cyclists.

- Create a movement that transforms how cycling is trained and coached.

Final Thoughts: The System™ is More Than a Program—It's a Movement.

I created The System™ because I knew there was a better way. A way that eliminates frustration, makes training clear and effective, and helps cyclists achieve long-term success instead of short-term gains.

If you're tired of:

- Training without a real system.

- Feeling stuck at a performance plateau.

- Following one-size-fits-all plans that don't deliver.

It's time to train smarter, not just harder. THE SYSTEM™ 6x6 ensures that training is structured, measurable, and continuously refined for long-term mastery.

"Mastery isn't about chasing numbers—it's about owning your performance, refining every detail, and transforming effort into excellence."

— Coach David

Chapter 1: The Origins of THE SYSTEM™

The Evolution of High-Performance Training

Every great system is born out of necessity. THE SYSTEM™ was no different. It emerged from a deep understanding of human physiology, training science, and the mental fortitude required to achieve elite performance. More than just a training methodology, THE SYSTEM™ is a framework designed to maximize an athlete's full potential by integrating endurance, power, mental resilience, and energy system mastery into a structured and repeatable process.

This chapter explores how THE SYSTEM™ came to life, the principles that shaped it, and why it continues revolutionizing training for cyclists and endurance athletes worldwide.

The Journey to THE SYSTEM™

The origins of THE SYSTEM™ can be traced back to Coach David's experiences as both an athlete and coach. Over the years, he worked with cyclists at every level—from beginners aiming to complete their first endurance ride to elite competitors pushing for podium finishes. One fundamental truth emerged through this journey: training methodologies often focused too narrowly on power or endurance, neglecting the holistic approach needed for sustained performance gains.

This realization led to the development of the 6x6 Framework— a training model designed to optimize all facets of performance rather than focusing on isolated metrics. The goal was simple: to create a system that would guide athletes to peak performance through a repeatable, data-driven, and adaptable approach.

The Influence of Martial Arts and Mental Conditioning

One of the biggest influences in shaping THE SYSTEM™ was not cycling alone but martial arts. Having trained in Cuong Nhu Oriental Martial Arts for over 25 years and achieving Black Belt status,

Coach David learned the significance of discipline, technique, and structured progression. Martial arts emphasize fluid movement, balance, energy efficiency, and mental resilience—all of which translate seamlessly into endurance sports.

This philosophy became a core tenet of THE SYSTEM™: progression is not just about numbers on a power meter but about developing the mindset and resilience to apply training effectively in competition and long-term athletic success.

Why THE SYSTEM™ Was Created

The driving force behind THE SYSTEM™ was to break down the intimidating complexity of elite training. Too often, athletes feel overwhelmed by scientific terminology, technical data, and intricate workout structures. This can lead to confusion, discouragement, and a sense of exclusion from the "elite" circle.

Coach David recognized that the core principles of elite training are not inherently complex—they have just been overcomplicated by the industry. In reality, these principles can be taught in a way that is simple, actionable, and universally applicable, empowering every athlete to train like a professional.

The Power of Simplicity

One of the most important elements of THE SYSTEM™ is its focus on simplifying complexity. This doesn't mean dumbing down the science; rather, it means presenting advanced training strategies in an easy-to-understand and implement way.

- No more jargon: Concepts like VO2 Max, lactate clearance, and cadence control are explained in straightforward language.

- Actionable guidance: Instead of abstract theories, athletes receive clear, actionable steps for implementation.

- Universal applicability: The strategies work whether you're a beginner or an elite competitor, ensuring that no one is left behind.

The Science Behind THE SYSTEM™

THE SYSTEM™ is deeply rooted in physiology, energy system management, and structured periodization. It is built on:

- Endurance Fundamentals – Developing an aerobic base for sustained performance.

- Energy System Mastery – Understanding how each system contributes to overall fitness.

- Neuromuscular Efficiency – Refining pedaling mechanics and force application.

- Effort Control & Mindfulness – Training with precision and intention.

- Mental Resilience – Strengthening the mind to handle the toughest challenges.

With the right combination of training structure, physiological adaptation, and mental engagement, THE SYSTEM™ allows athletes to reach peak fitness while avoiding burnout, maximizing performance longevity, and maintaining a data-driven approach to progression.

Breaking Down Barriers to Elite Training

In the world of high-performance sports, elite-level training is often seen as exclusive and unattainable, reserved for professionals with access to advanced coaches, expensive tools, and complex data analytics. The narrative suggests that only a select few can truly understand and benefit from the secrets of peak performance. But what if that weren't true?

THE SYSTEM™ was created to demystify elite-level training, making it accessible to athletes of all levels. The vision is simple yet revolutionary: anyone—from beginners to seasoned competitors—can access the same elite strategies without the jargon that dominates mainstream training conversations.

A Mission of Inclusivity and Accessibility

THE SYSTEM™ was created with a purpose far beyond just optimizing athletic performance. It was designed to break down barriers of exclusivity in elite-level training, ensuring that advanced performance strategies are accessible to everyone—regardless of race, background, or experience level.

This mission is deeply rooted in Coach David's extensive experience as the Past DEI Director at USA Cycling and his years of Thought Leadership in the Corporate Banking Sector. Through his journey, he recognized the need for a training system that not only empowers athletes but also erases color lines and makes cycling, training, and performance inclusive for all, not just for a select few.

- Breaking Down Racial Barriers: THE SYSTEM™ aims to bridge the gap in cycling and endurance sports, where historically, People of Color have been underrepresented.

- Empowering Underrepresented Communities: By providing knowledge, resources, and a supportive community, THE SYSTEM™ levels the playing field, ensuring that all athletes have an equal opportunity to excel.

- Redefining the Culture of Cycling and Performance: This approach goes beyond training; it's about creating a cultural shift that celebrates diversity, inclusion, and equitable access to high-performance coaching.

The Road Ahead

This book takes you through every facet of THE SYSTEM™ 6x6 Framework, breaking down each of its six core areas into Training Elements, Energy Systems, Performance Standards, Core Training Philosophies, EQ-i® Skills, and Leadership Elements.

As we move through each chapter, you'll gain an in-depth understanding of how to apply these principles in your own training, whether you're a cyclist, endurance athlete, or coach looking to implement a proven system for long-term success.

This is not just a training methodology; it's a movement to redefine what it means to train like an elite.

Next Chapter: Mastering the 6 Training Elements

Now that we've laid the groundwork, let's dive into the first core component of THE SYSTEM™: The 6 Training Elements and how they drive peak performance.

Chapter 2: Mastering the 6 Training Elements

The Foundation of Performance

Training is more than just logging miles or increasing power numbers. It is about developing a structured and progressive approach that integrates multiple physiological and technical components. THE SYSTEM™ 6 Training Elements are the foundation upon which all performance improvements are built. Each element serves a unique role in the development of an athlete, ensuring balanced growth and peak fitness.

These elements are not independent; they are interwoven, affecting and influencing each other. Mastering them requires patience, consistency, and a strategic approach.

The Purpose Behind the Training Elements

The 6 Training Elements of THE SYSTEM™ were meticulously crafted to provide a comprehensive, repeatable, and adaptable structure that caters to every level of athlete. From beginners building their aerobic base to elite competitors fine-tuning their explosive power, these elements ensure that no stone is left unturned.

In traditional training methodologies, athletes often focus too narrowly on isolated aspects such as endurance or power. This fragmented approach leads to imbalances and plateaus, preventing athletes from reaching their full potential. In contrast, THE SYSTEM™ provides a holistic framework that integrates all aspects of performance.

- **Endurance Training** builds the aerobic engine necessary for sustained performance.

- **Cadence Control** enhances efficiency and neuromuscular coordination.

- **Force/Tempo Development** bridges strength and endurance, ensuring consistent power output.

- **Speed Endurance** increases the ability to sustain high velocities over prolonged periods.

- **Power Generation** unlocks explosive efforts crucial for sprints and attacks.

- **Threshold/Lactate Clearance** improves resistance to fatigue and extends sustained effort capabilities.

The magic of **THE SYSTEM™** lies not only in mastering each element but also in understanding **how they interact and influence each other.** This interconnectedness ensures balanced development and long-term progression.

The 6 Training Elements

1. Endurance Training – The Engine of Performance

Endurance is the backbone of all athletic performance. It determines how long you can sustain efforts and how well you recover between high-intensity efforts.

- Focuses on aerobic development, increasing oxygen delivery to muscles.

- Builds efficiency in fat metabolism and energy utilization.

- Essential for long-duration events, recovery, and sustainability.

- Training methods: Zone 2 endurance rides, long, steady efforts, and controlled pacing.

2. Cadence Control – Efficiency in Motion

Cadence is more than just pedal speed; it is about efficiency and control. Mastering cadence allows an athlete to apply power in a way that optimizes energy use.

- Involves refining pedal stroke to eliminate inefficiencies.

- Enhances neuromuscular coordination and power application.

- Reduces unnecessary fatigue by maintaining optimal muscle recruitment.

- Training methods: High-cadence drills, low-cadence force work, and terrain-specific cadence practice.

3. Force/Tempo Development – Strength Meets Stamina

Force and tempo development ensure an athlete can generate and sustain power effectively, especially in varying terrain and tactical race situations.

- Builds muscular endurance for sustained efforts.

- Strengthens the ability to maintain power output over extended periods.

- Bridges the gap between endurance and high-intensity work.

- Training methods: Sweet spot intervals, big-gear hill repeats, and progressive overload training.

4. Speed Endurance – The Ability to Sustain High Velocities

Speed endurance training focuses on maintaining high speeds for prolonged efforts, crucial for breakaways, time trials, and finishing strong in races.

- Develops resistance to fatigue at high intensities.

- Enhances anaerobic capacity and lactate tolerance.

- Trains the body to recover quickly from surges.

- Training methods: Over/under intervals, race-pace simulations, and progressive sprint drills.

5. Power Generation – Unlocking Explosiveness

Power generation is the ability to produce high-output efforts efficiently. This element focuses on improving peak power and explosive strength.

- Essential for sprinting, climbing, and closing gaps in races.

- Trains fast-twitch muscle fibers for maximum force production.

- Improves reaction time and ability to respond to race dynamics.

- Training methods: Sprint intervals, high-wattage accelerations, and neuromuscular activation exercises.

6. Threshold/Lactate Clearance – The Art of Sustained Power

Lactate clearance training enhances an athlete's ability to manage fatigue and push harder for longer without hitting a breaking point.

- Improves sustained power output at lactate threshold.

- Increases efficiency in lactate buffering and removal.

- Develops ability to hold race pace for extended efforts.

- Training methods: Functional threshold power (FTP) intervals, long sub-threshold efforts, and race-pace simulations.

How These Elements Work Together

The beauty of THE SYSTEM™ is that these elements do not function in isolation. A well-structured training program integrates all six elements seamlessly, ensuring an athlete develops holistically rather than excelling in one area while neglecting another.

- Endurance Training supports recovery and enables more extensive high-intensity work.

- Cadence Control optimizes energy use and neuromuscular coordination.

- Force/Tempo Development bridges strength and endurance.

- Speed Endurance ensures the ability to sustain intensity.

- Power Generation improves race-day explosiveness.

- Threshold/Lactate Clearance develops resistance to fatigue and extends sustained effort capabilities.

By mastering these elements systematically and progressively, an athlete can reach their peak performance and sustain it over time.

Next Chapter: Energy System Mastery

With a deep understanding of the training elements, we now shift focus to how the body generates and sustains energy during performance. In the next chapter, we will break down the 6 Energy Systems, explaining how each contributes to cycling performance and how to train them effectively.

Chapter 3: Energy System Mastery

Unlocking the Power of Your Energy Systems

Every athletic performance is fueled by energy, and understanding how the body generates and sustains that energy is crucial for maximizing performance. In THE SYSTEM™ 6x6 Framework, the six energy systems play a pivotal role in determining an athlete's ability to execute sustained efforts, explosive sprints, and efficient recoveries.

Unlike traditional training approaches that emphasize singular aspects of performance, THE SYSTEM™ ensures that all energy systems are developed in harmony. This integration allows athletes to build a foundation that supports both endurance-based efforts and short bursts of high-intensity power.

This chapter will break down the 6 Energy Systems, explaining how each one contributes to endurance, power, and recovery, along with training strategies to optimize them. Each energy system has a specific role, but the key to high performance lies in training them synergistically so they work together effectively.

- **Pmax (Peak Power Output):** The maximum force an athlete can generate in a short explosive effort, essential for sprinting and surges.

- **VO2 Max (Maximal Oxygen Uptake):** The body's ability to use oxygen efficiently during high-intensity efforts is crucial for sustaining hard efforts.

- **TTE (Time to Exhaustion):** The duration an athlete can sustain a given power level, which directly impacts endurance.

- **FRC (Functional Reserve Capacity):** The anaerobic energy available above FTP determines how long an athlete can sustain power bursts before fatigue sets in.

- **MFTP (Maximal Functional Threshold Power):** The highest power output an athlete can maintain for an extended period without rapid fatigue.

- **Stamina:** The ability to sustain efforts over long durations with minimal fatigue, ensuring endurance, strength, and resilience.

To truly master performance, an athlete must develop all six energy systems through structured training that strategically balances intensity, recovery, and adaptation.

The 6 Energy Systems

1. Pmax (Peak Power Output) – Explosive Strength and Acceleration

Pmax represents an athlete's ability to generate maximum force in the shortest time possible. It is the foundation of sprinting, launching attacks, and short bursts of power.

- Key physiological focus: Neuromuscular recruitment, phosphocreatine stores, and fast-twitch muscle fiber activation.

- Training methods: Short sprints (5-10 seconds), standing start accelerations, high-torque efforts, and maximal power efforts.

2. VO2 Max (Maximal Oxygen Uptake) – Sustained High-Intensity Performance

VO2 Max is the body's ability to consume and utilize oxygen efficiently at high intensities. It determines an athlete's aerobic ceiling and influences endurance performance.

- Key physiological focus: Aerobic capacity, cardiovascular efficiency, and oxygen transport.

- Training methods: VO2 Max intervals (3-6 minutes at 90-95% max effort), hill repeats, and over/under intervals.

3. TTE (Time to Exhaustion) – Holding Power Over Time

TTE is the measure of how long an athlete can sustain a given power level, particularly around threshold intensity. This directly impacts long-duration performance and pacing strategies.

- Key physiological focus: Lactate threshold development, aerobic endurance, and energy system efficiency.

- Training methods: Long sub-threshold intervals, sustained tempo efforts, and negative-split endurance rides.

4. FRC (Functional Reserve Capacity) – The Anaerobic Energy Buffer

FRC represents the energy available above Functional Threshold Power (FTP) before exhaustion. It is crucial for repeated surges, breakaways, and short efforts that exceed the threshold.

- Key physiological focus: Anaerobic power, lactate tolerance, and fast-twitch fiber endurance.

- Training methods: Repeated anaerobic efforts (30 seconds to 2 minutes), Tabata-style intervals, and race-simulation surges.

5. MFTP (Maximal Functional Threshold Power) – The Benchmark for Sustained Efforts

MFTP, commonly referred to as FTP, is an athlete's sustainable power output for extended durations. It serves as the foundation for pacing in endurance events.

- Key physiological focus: Aerobic efficiency, muscular endurance, and metabolic adaptation.

- Training methods: FTP intervals (8-20 minutes), progressive over/under sets, and race-pace simulations.

6. Stamina – The Ability to Go the Distance

Stamina is an athlete's ability to maintain efforts over prolonged durations with minimal fatigue. It encompasses endurance capacity and recovery efficiency.

- Key physiological focus: Fat metabolism, glycogen conservation, and long-term endurance adaptations.

- Training methods: Long endurance rides, low-intensity high-volume training (LIT), and steady-state tempo rides.

Training Strategies for Energy System Optimization

Each energy system must be trained strategically to improve overall performance. While they work in conjunction with one another, targeted training ensures maximum efficiency and adaptation.

- Periodized Training: Structuring training blocks to focus on specific energy systems at different points in the season.

- Hybrid Workouts: Combining elements of endurance, power, and anaerobic efforts within a single session to simulate race demands.

- Recovery Focus: Ensuring proper rest between high-intensity efforts to allow for full system adaptation.

- Data-Driven Adjustments: Using performance metrics to track improvements and modify training intensity as needed.

How the 6 Energy Systems Work Together

The interaction between these energy systems is what makes THE SYSTEM™ so effective. For example:

- A strong Pmax allows for explosive starts and powerful sprints.

- High VO2 Max supports sustained efforts at race intensity.

- TTE and MFTP ensure the ability to hold power over time.

- FRC enables repeated accelerations without immediate exhaustion.

- Stamina ensures long-term efficiency and resilience in endurance events.

By mastering these six energy systems, athletes can train smarter, perform stronger, and sustain peak performance longer.

Next Chapter: Prime Level Performance Standards

Now that we've explored how the body produces energy, we turn to the 6 Prime Level Performance Standards, which define the mental and physical attributes needed to push beyond limits and achieve breakthrough performance.

Chapter 4: Prime Level Performance Standards

The Pillars of Elite Performance

Achieving peak performance is not solely dependent on physical training; it is equally a mental and emotional endeavor. THE SYSTEM™ 6x6 Framework incorporates 6 Prime Level Performance Standards, which define the core attributes needed to push past limitations and sustain excellence in training and competition.

These six standards serve as guiding principles, shaping how athletes approach training, competition, and personal growth. When cultivated properly, they create a mindset and work ethic that separate elite performers from the rest. Athletes who master these standards become not just physically strong but also mentally resilient, capable of overcoming setbacks, adapting to challenges, and executing under pressure.

The Prime Level Performance Standards include:

1. Drive – The intrinsic motivation to push beyond limits.

2. Confidence – The belief in one's ability to achieve goals.

3. Intensity – The ability to sustain high effort over time.

4. Focus – The ability to concentrate on the task at hand.

5. Emotion – The capacity to manage and channel emotions productively.

6. Mental Resilience – The strength to overcome challenges and setbacks.

By integrating these six standards into training, athletes develop not just the physical endurance needed for competition but also the mental fortitude required to excel under pressure.

The 6 Prime Level Performance Standards

1. Drive – The Will to Push Beyond Limits

The drive is the intrinsic motivation that fuels continuous improvement. It is the relentless pursuit of progress, the hunger to achieve goals, and the refusal to settle for mediocrity.

- Why it matters: Without drive, training becomes stagnant, and performance plateaus.

- How to develop it: Set ambitious but realistic goals, create a roadmap for success, and visualize achieving milestones.

2. Confidence – The Belief in Your Abilities

Confidence is the unwavering belief in one's ability to execute under pressure. It is built through preparation, consistency, and self-assurance.

- Why it matters: Confidence turns training into execution and potential into results.

- How to develop it: Focus on small victories, analyze past successes, and reinforce positive self-talk.

3. Intensity – The Capacity to Maintain Effort Over Time

Intensity is the ability to sustain high levels of effort, whether in training or competition. It is about controlled aggression and applying the right amount of force at the right moments.

- Why it matters: Without intensity, workouts lack effectiveness, and races become survival rather than performance.

- How to develop it: Incorporate high-intensity interval training, push beyond comfort zones, and embrace competitive settings.

4. Focus – The Power of Present-Moment Awareness

Focus is the ability to eliminate distractions and maintain concentration on the task at hand. It is essential for executing race strategies and maintaining consistency in training.

- Why it matters: A lack of focus leads to mistakes, inefficient energy use, and missed opportunities.

- How to develop it: Practice mindfulness, use cue words during workouts, and create pre-race routines.

5. Emotion – The Ability to Harness Passion for Performance

Emotion plays a critical role in performance, whether it is channeling excitement, managing nerves, or rebounding from setbacks. Learning to control emotions enhances mental toughness.

- Why it matters: Emotion can be a tool for motivation or a downfall if not managed correctly.

- How to develop it: Recognize emotional triggers, develop stress-management techniques, and use emotions constructively.

6. Mental Resilience – The Strength to Overcome Challenges

Mental resilience is the ability to recover from setbacks, push through adversity, and stay committed despite obstacles. It is the defining trait of champions.

- Why it matters: Training and competition come with highs and lows. Those who persist through challenges find the most success.

- How to develop it: Embrace challenges as learning opportunities, maintain perspective, and cultivate a growth mindset.

Integrating the 6 Prime Level Performance Standards into Training

While these standards may seem intangible, they can be actively trained and reinforced just like physical attributes.

1. Develop a Personal Performance Mindset

- Set clear goals and remind yourself of your 'why.'

- Create routines that reinforce confidence and focus.

2. Implement Mental Conditioning Exercises

- Use visualization techniques before workouts and races.
- Practice mindfulness to stay present during key efforts.

3. Establish Accountability and Reflection Practices

- Track emotional and mental responses in a training journal.
- Regularly assess progress in each of the six standards.

4. Surround Yourself with a High-Performance Environment

- Train with individuals who push you beyond your comfort zone.
- Seek guidance from coaches who emphasize both physical and mental development.

How These Standards Elevate Performance

Athletes who cultivate these standards experience:

✓ Increased resilience in the face of adversity.

✓ Enhanced consistency and focus during training and competition.

✓ Greater ability to execute under high-pressure scenarios.

✓ Long-term sustainability in both motivation and results.

By developing these traits, an athlete moves beyond just being physically prepared—they become mentally unshakable and emotionally balanced.

Next Chapter: Core Training Philosophies

With a strong understanding of both physical training and mental performance, we now explore the 6 Core Training Philosophies that form the foundation of THE SYSTEM™. These philosophies ensure that training is structured, efficient, and sustainable for long-term progression.

Chapter 5: Core Training Philosophies

Building the Framework for Sustainable Success

Long-term success in athletic performance goes beyond individual workouts or short-term goals. It requires a strategic, disciplined, and sustainable approach that not only enhances fitness but also fosters mental resilience and efficient recovery. While training methodologies and data-driven performance metrics are crucial, true mastery is built upon foundational principles that guide progress over months and years—not just weeks.

THE SYSTEM™ 6 Core Training Philosophies serve as the framework for structured development, ensuring that every athlete moves forward with purpose. By balancing structured effort with intelligent recovery, athletes can prevent overtraining, maximize performance longevity, and continue improving in a sustainable manner.

This approach isn't about merely pushing harder—it's about training smarter. Athletes who embrace these philosophies understand that success is a combination of physical preparedness, mental fortitude, and long-term strategic execution.

The 6 Core Training Philosophies of THE SYSTEM™ ensure that every aspect of training—from effort execution to recovery—is intentional and sustainable:

1. Discipline and Consistency – Establishing structured habits and a long-term training approach.

2. Effort Control and Mindful Execution – Training with purpose and intentional effort.

3. Adaptability and Resilience – Adjusting to training demands and overcoming challenges.

4. Continuous Learning and Growth – Refining strategies based on experience and data.

5. Energy System Mastery – Training all physiological systems for balanced development.

6. Balance and Recovery – Integrating smart recovery to sustain peak performance.

By incorporating these philosophies, athletes create a strong foundation for success—one that fosters continuous improvement while reducing the risk of injury and burnout. The journey to peak performance isn't just about how hard you train but how well you train over time.

While training methodologies and data-driven performance metrics are crucial, true long-term success is built on a foundation of core training philosophies. These principles ensure that every athlete progresses efficiently, minimizes injury risk, and sustains peak performance over time.

THE SYSTEM™ 6 Core Training Philosophies provide the structure needed to develop an athlete beyond just physical capability. They focus on discipline, precision, adaptability, continuous improvement, and recovery.

Elite athletes are not simply those who can generate the highest power numbers or log the most training hours; they are those who train with purpose, consistency, and strategic intent. Without a structured approach that balances effort and recovery, athletes often plateau, suffer from overtraining or fail to reach their true potential.

The 6 Core Training Philosophies

1. Discipline and Consistency – The Bedrock of Progress

Elite performance is not built in a day; it requires structured, repetitive, and purposeful training. Consistency is key to reinforcing physiological adaptations and skill development.

- Why it matters: Training success is not about one great session but about stacking small wins over time.

- How to develop it: Establish a structured training routine, set process-oriented goals, and prioritize daily execution.

2. Effort Control and Mindful Execution – Train with Precision

Understanding how to regulate effort and precisely execute workouts ensures optimal adaptation while avoiding burnout.

- Why it matters: Random efforts lead to random results. Measured effort leads to sustainable gains.

- How to develop it: Use heart rate, power zones, and perceived effort as guides. Maintain focus on form and execution in every session.

3. Adaptability and Resilience – Training for the Unexpected

Training and competition rarely go as planned. The ability to adapt and adjust to new challenges is what separates good athletes from great ones.

- Why it matters: Adapting to setbacks ensures consistent progress even in less-than-ideal conditions.

- How to develop it: Learn to modify training based on external factors (weather, fatigue, life stress) without compromising long-term goals.

4. Continuous Learning and Growth – The Pursuit of Mastery

Every session is an opportunity to learn. Athletes must seek ongoing education in training principles, nutrition, and mindset strategies.

- Why it matters: Stagnation occurs when athletes stop evolving and refining their approach.

- How to develop it: Analyze training data, seek feedback from coaches, and engage with educational resources to refine performance strategies.

5. Energy System Mastery – Understanding the Body's Power Sources

Training should be structured to develop all energy systems efficiently, ensuring a well-rounded and complete performance profile.

- Why it matters: A balanced approach prevents weaknesses and maximizes performance in all cycling disciplines.

- How to develop it: Tailor training blocks to address endurance, power, and recovery components systematically.

6. Balance and Recovery – The Foundation of Longevity

Recovery is often the most overlooked component of training. Without it, adaptations cannot occur, and performance deteriorates.

- Why it matters: Overtraining leads to diminishing returns, burnout, and increased injury risk.

- How to develop it: Implement structured recovery blocks, prioritize sleep, and listen to biofeedback for fatigue management.

Applying These Philosophies in Training

To integrate these philosophies into daily practice, athletes should:

- Develop a structured training plan that accounts for periodization and progressive overload.

- Maintain a training journal to track progress, highlight lessons, and refine execution.

- Incorporate self-assessment strategies to adjust training intensity and volume based on performance trends.

- Use coach feedback and peer insights to maintain accountability and direction.

How These Philosophies Drive Sustainable Performance

By aligning training with these six philosophies, athletes experience:

✓ Reduced burnout and overtraining risk

✓ Increased ability to adapt and optimize training

✓ Greater consistency in performance execution

✓ A holistic, long-term approach to fitness and endurance development

Next Chapter: Emotional Intelligence in Performance

With a solid foundation in training philosophy, the next step is understanding the role of emotional intelligence in performance. Chapter 6 will explore how self-awareness, emotional control, and mental resilience contribute to elite athletic success.

Chapter 6: Emotional Intelligence in Performance

The Role of Emotional Intelligence in Athletic Success

In high-performance training, physical preparation is only half the equation. The ability to manage emotions, make clear decisions under pressure, and maintain composure during adversity separates great athletes from the rest. Emotional Intelligence (EQ) plays a crucial role in an athlete's resilience, motivation, and ability to execute strategies effectively.

Athletes who develop emotional intelligence can better handle setbacks, maintain focus, and regulate stress levels during competition and training. It is not just about training the body; it is about training the mind to respond to challenges with calmness, confidence, and clarity.

Emotional intelligence impacts every aspect of performance, from how an athlete approaches high-pressure race moments to their ability to stay engaged in long-term training cycles without burnout. Those who master EQ can quickly shift from frustration to focus, turning obstacles into opportunities for growth.

In THE SYSTEM™ 6x6 Framework, emotional intelligence is structured around six key EQ-i® skills that enhance both training and competition:

1. Self-Regard – Developing confidence in one's own abilities and potential.

2. Self-Actualization – The continuous drive for self-improvement and mastery.

3. Emotional Self-Awareness – Understanding emotions and how they affect performance.

4. Independence – The ability to make strong, confident decisions without external validation.

24

5. Impulse Control – Managing emotional reactions and maintaining composure under pressure.

6. Stress Tolerance – The ability to perform effectively in high-stress environments.

By integrating these EQ skills into training, athletes develop a mental edge that complements their physical conditioning, allowing them to thrive in competition, training, and everyday life.

The 6 EQ-i® Skills for Performance

1. Self-Regard – Confidence in One's Abilities

Self-regard is the ability to recognize and appreciate personal strengths and weaknesses. Athletes with strong self-regard believe in their training and trust their capabilities in competition.

- Why it matters: Confidence leads to better decision-making and risk-taking in races.

- How to develop it: Reflect on past successes, maintain positive self-talk, and set process-driven goals.

2. Self-Actualization – Continuous Growth and Mastery

Self-actualization is the drive to reach one's full potential. It fuels an athlete's motivation and willingness to invest in long-term progress.

- Why it matters: Athletes who focus on mastery and personal growth stay committed and adaptable.

- How to develop it: Set meaningful long-term goals, engage in deliberate practice, and seek continuous learning opportunities.

3. Emotional Self-Awareness – Recognizing and Managing Emotions

Emotional self-awareness allows athletes to understand how their emotions impact performance. Recognizing stress, anxiety, or excitement helps in developing strategies to regulate them.

- Why it matters: Controlling emotions prevents distractions and maintains mental clarity.

- How to develop it: Practice mindfulness, track emotional responses in training, and implement pre-race routines.

4. Independence – Self-Reliance in Training and Competition

Independence is the ability to make confident decisions without excessive reliance on others. It allows athletes to take ownership of their training and race strategies.

- Why it matters: Self-reliant athletes adapt quickly in races and handle unexpected challenges effectively.

- How to develop it: Learn from mistakes, trust personal judgment, and analyze race situations independently.

5. Impulse Control – Managing Reactions Under Pressure

Impulse control is the ability to regulate immediate reactions and avoid making emotionally driven decisions that could hinder performance.

- Why it matters: Controlling impulses leads to better pacing, race tactics, and energy conservation.

- How to develop it: Use breathing techniques, practice controlled effort execution, and develop mental discipline through structured training.

6. Stress Tolerance – Performing Under Pressure

Stress tolerance is the ability to maintain focus and performance in high-pressure situations. It ensures that an athlete remains composed when facing adversity.

- Why it matters: Endurance sports and competition demand the ability to thrive under stress.

- How to develop it: Simulate race-day stress in training, visualize success under pressure, and build routines reinforcing mental stability.

Integrating Emotional Intelligence into Training

To harness the power of EQ in training and racing, athletes should:

- Develop Pre-Race and Pre-Workout Rituals to reinforce emotional control.

- Maintain a Performance Journal to track emotional responses and identify patterns.

- Use Visualization Techniques to rehearse success and overcome challenges mentally.

- Engage in Breathwork and Mindfulness Practices to manage stress and improve focus.

How EQ Enhances Athletic Performance

Athletes who prioritize emotional intelligence experience:

✓ Improved mental resilience and adaptability

✓ Greater consistency in performance under pressure

✓ Enhanced ability to make strategic decisions in competition

✓ Increased confidence and self-efficacy in high-stakes moments

Next Chapter: Leadership in Training and Competition

With emotional intelligence as the foundation for mental performance, the next step is understanding how leadership traits influence success in training and competition. Chapter 7 explores the 6 Leadership Elements that define high-performing athletes and coaches.

Chapter 7: Leadership in Training and Competition

The Role of Leadership in Athletic Success

Leadership is not limited to team captains or coaches—it is a quality that every athlete can cultivate. True leaders inspire those around them, maintain accountability, and exhibit resilience in the face of adversity. Leadership is about setting an example through discipline, consistency, and strategic decision-making, both in training and competition.

In endurance sports, leadership extends beyond motivating teammates—it also means taking ownership of one's own performance, making smart tactical choices, and learning how to adapt under pressure. A strong leader understands that progress requires self-discipline, vision, and the ability to execute under stress.

Athletes who develop leadership skills see improvements in their ability to train efficiently, execute race strategies with confidence, and manage setbacks effectively. Leadership is not just about guiding others; it is about mastering oneself first.

Within THE SYSTEM™ 6x6 Framework, leadership is defined by six core elements that influence both individual and team success:

1. Vision – Setting clear goals and maintaining focus on long-term development.

2. Accountability – Taking responsibility for training, execution, and results.

3. Communication – Effectively conveying ideas, strategies, and feedback.

4. Adaptability – Adjusting to challenges, setbacks, and unpredictable race conditions.

5. Influence – Inspiring and motivating others through actions and mindset.

6. Resilience – Maintaining strength, persistence, and composure through adversity.

By integrating these leadership principles into daily training and competition, athletes develop the ability to lead by example, make intelligent tactical decisions, and create a high-performance environment around them. Leadership is not about a title—it is about taking ownership of the journey and striving for continuous excellence.

The 6 Leadership Elements

1. Vision – Setting Clear Goals and Strategies

Vision provides direction and purpose in an athlete's journey. Leaders create a roadmap for their success and inspire others to align with long-term objectives.

- Why it matters: Without a clear vision, training lacks structure, and motivation diminishes.

- How to develop it: Set SMART goals (Specific, Measurable, Achievable, Relevant, Time-bound) and consistently review progress.

2. Accountability – Taking Ownership of Performance

Accountability ensures that athletes take responsibility for their training, execution, and results. Leaders do not blame external factors; they adapt and find solutions.

- Why it matters: Ownership leads to continuous self-improvement and resilience.

- How to develop it: Track progress in a training journal, analyze performance data and embrace constructive feedback.

3. Communication – Effectively Conveying Ideas and Feedback

Strong communication skills allow athletes to express their needs, share insights, and contribute to a collaborative training environment.

- Why it matters: Effective communication strengthens teamwork and coach-athlete relationships.

- How to develop it: Practice active listening, provide clear feedback, and engage in open discussions with teammates and coaches.

4. Adaptability – Adjusting to Challenges and Changing Conditions

Adaptability is the ability to modify strategies based on circumstances such as race conditions, training setbacks, or unexpected challenges.

- Why it matters: Rigid athletes struggle to progress, whereas adaptable ones thrive in changing environments.

- How to develop it: Embrace flexible training plans, learn from failures, and maintain a growth mindset.

5. Influence – Inspiring and Motivating Others

Great athletes lead by example. They inspire teammates and create a culture of excellence through their work ethic and attitude.

- Why it matters: A strong influence can elevate team performance and foster a supportive environment.

- How to develop it: Demonstrate discipline, encourage others, and celebrate team successes.

6. Resilience – Maintaining Strength Through Adversity

Resilience is the ability to stay composed and push forward despite obstacles. It is the hallmark of champions who overcome setbacks and maintain peak performance.

- Why it matters: Resilience ensures longevity in the sport and sustains motivation during difficult times.

- How to develop it: Practice mental conditioning, develop pre-race stress management techniques, and reframe setbacks as learning opportunities.

Integrating Leadership into Training and Competition

To cultivate leadership skills, athletes should:

● Establish daily habits that reinforce responsibility and discipline.

● Engage in team-based activities to enhance collaboration and mentorship.

● Seek opportunities for self-reflection to refine leadership qualities.

● Maintain a strong mental approach by embracing challenges and staying solution-focused.

How Leadership Elevates Performance

Athletes who develop leadership qualities experience:

✓ Greater confidence in race-day decision-making

✓ Improved teamwork and communication with coaches and peers

✓ Stronger resilience and adaptability in unpredictable situations

✓ Enhanced motivation and accountability for long-term success

Next Chapter: The Road to Mastery

Leadership sets the stage for long-term success, but true mastery requires a commitment to lifelong improvement. Chapter 8 explores the final integration of THE SYSTEM™ 6x6 Framework, ensuring that athletes maximize their potential and sustain peak performance.

Chapter 8: The Road to Mastery

The Journey Toward Peak Performance

Mastery in any discipline is not a destination but an ongoing process of refinement, adaptation, and dedication. The journey to peak performance is built on consistent progress, structured training, and a mindset focused on continual improvement.

THE SYSTEM™ 6x6 Framework is designed to create a pathway for athletes to sustain long-term growth, optimize performance, and push beyond self-imposed limitations. Unlike traditional training methodologies that focus only on isolated components of performance, THE SYSTEM™ integrates physical, mental, and strategic development to ensure complete mastery over time.

True mastery requires an athlete to not only develop raw fitness and power but also to understand how to execute under pressure, sustain peak performance across different energy systems, and maintain a resilient and disciplined mindset.

This chapter explores how to integrate all aspects of:

- **The 6 Training Elements** – Developing endurance, cadence control, force, speed, power, and lactate clearance.

- **The 6 Energy Systems** – Understanding how the body generates and utilizes energy for sustained performance.

- **The 6 Prime Level Performance Standards** – Cultivating drive, confidence, intensity, focus, emotion, and mental resilience.

- **The 6 Core Training Philosophies** – Ensuring discipline, effort control, adaptability, continuous learning, energy system mastery, and balance.

- **The 6 EQ-i® Skills** – Harnessing emotional intelligence for self-awareness, stress tolerance, and peak execution.

- **The 6 Leadership Elements** – Building vision, accountability, communication, adaptability, influence, and resilience.

Athletes create a comprehensive blueprint for sustainable success by applying these principles together. The pursuit of peak performance is not about perfection—it's about continuous refinement and staying engaged in the process of growth.

Mastery is not just about training harder but training smarter with purpose, patience, and a strategic approach. The road to peak performance is an evolving path, and THE SYSTEM™ ensures that every athlete has the structure and knowledge to reach their highest potential.

The Phases of Mastery

1. Foundation – Building a Strong Base

Mastery starts with understanding the fundamental elements of training, energy systems, and mental resilience.

- Key focus: Developing endurance, strength, and technical skills.

- How to apply: Follow structured training plans, build consistent habits, and establish a strong mindset.

2. Progression – Advancing Training and Execution

Once the foundation is set, progression involves refining skills, increasing intensity, and optimizing efficiency.

- Key focus: Adapting training to improve performance markers.

- How to apply: Utilize data analysis, refine technique, and implement progressive overload.

3. Adaptation – Adjusting to Challenges and Growth

True mastery requires adaptability in training, competition, and recovery.

- Key focus: Managing setbacks, adjusting strategies, and ensuring long-term progression.

- How to apply: Modify training plans based on biofeedback, recovery metrics, and life stressors.

4. Execution – Performing at Peak Levels

Execution is about consistently delivering high-level performance when it matters most.

- Key focus: Mental toughness, strategic planning, and refined race-day execution.

- How to apply: Develop pre-race routines, train under competitive conditions, and simulate real-world challenges.

5. Innovation – Pushing Boundaries and Breaking Plateaus

Mastery involves constant evolution and the pursuit of innovation in training methods, techniques, and recovery strategies.

- Key focus: Experimenting with new techniques, incorporating cutting-edge training modalities.

- How to apply: Work with coaches, analyze trends and embrace emerging sports science advancements.

6. Sustainability – Longevity in Performance

The final stage of mastery is ensuring sustainability in training, health, and personal fulfillment.

- Key focus: Preventing burnout, maintaining motivation, and balancing training with life.

- How to apply: Prioritize recovery, set long-term goals, and foster a passion-driven approach to training.

Integrating THE SYSTEM™ for Lifelong Success

To achieve and sustain mastery, athletes should:

- Regularly assess progress and adjust training based on performance metrics.

- Commit to continuous learning by studying new training methodologies and techniques.

- Engage in self-reflection to understand strengths, weaknesses, and areas for growth.

- Cultivate resilience to push through challenges and maintain long-term success.

What If The System 6x6 Framework Did Not Exist?

What if THE SYSTEM™ 6x6 Framework had never been developed? Athletes might still rely on fragmented training methodologies, focusing solely on power or endurance without the integration of holistic performance elements.

- Without Endurance Training, long-distance efforts would suffer, leading to diminished stamina and recovery abilities.

- Without Cadence Control, inefficient pedaling mechanics could drain energy and reduce power output.

- Without Power Generation, athletes would struggle with explosive efforts, limiting their sprinting and acceleration capabilities.

- Mental resilience would be compromised without Emotional Intelligence Training, making it difficult to push through adversity in races and training.

- Without Leadership Elements, athletes might lack vision, accountability, and the ability to inspire and influence teammates.

- Without Energy System Mastery, workouts would lack precision, preventing athletes from maximizing their physiological potential.

The 6x6 Framework ensures a scientific, repeatable, and adaptable system that allows athletes to achieve and sustain peak performance. Without it, many would struggle with inconsistency, plateaus, and burnout, never unlocking their full potential. Fortunately, THE SYSTEM™ exists—empowering athletes to elevate their training and redefine their limits.

The Final Step: Becoming a Master of THE SYSTEM™

Athletes who commit to mastering THE SYSTEM™ 6x6 Framework experience:

✓ Greater consistency in training and performance.

✓ A refined ability to adapt and grow beyond plateaus.

✓ Enhanced self-awareness and leadership within the sport.

✓ A lifelong commitment to progression and peak performance.

Mastery is not about perfection; it is about continuous refinement, execution, and pushing beyond limits to create a legacy of performance excellence.

Conclusion: The Legacy of THE SYSTEM™

Mastering this framework goes beyond athletic performance—it influences mindset, discipline, and leadership. The principles within THE SYSTEM™ are designed to foster long-term development, resilience, and excellence across all facets of training and life.

Chapter 9: How We Use THE SYSTEM™

for Peak Performance

Applying THE SYSTEM™ in Training and Competition

THE SYSTEM™ is more than just a framework—it's a proven methodology that helps athletes consistently reach peak performance by aligning training with physiological principles, data-driven insights, and strategic execution. From structured training plans to real-world application, this chapter explores how to implement THE SYSTEM™ effectively in various scenarios, including endurance racing, time trials, and high-intensity competitions.

Athletes who follow THE SYSTEM™ understand that success is not about training harder—it's about training smarter. By integrating data-driven decision-making with holistic training strategies, THE SYSTEM™ provides the blueprint for:

- **Maximizing efficiency** in training and race execution.

- **Improving recovery** to sustain long-term performance.

- **Enhancing adaptation** to build fitness without burnout progressively.

- **Applying energy system mastery** to specific race demands.

- **Balancing effort control and intensity** for peak competition readiness.

How to Implement THE SYSTEM™

1. Structured Training Progression – Follow a periodized approach that progressively builds endurance, strength, and peak power while avoiding overtraining.

2. Energy System Optimization – Train each energy system strategically to match race-day demands, ensuring readiness for different competition types.

3. Data-Driven Adjustments – Use performance analytics to refine training loads, recovery periods, and intensity zones.

4. Mental and Emotional Preparedness – Develop confidence, focus, and emotional resilience to execute under race pressure.

5. Tactical Race Execution – Apply training principles in real-world scenarios, leveraging pacing strategies, surges, and recovery to gain a competitive edge.

By applying THE SYSTEM™ intelligently, athletes create consistency in performance, sustain peak fitness throughout the season, and continually improve year over year. The path to elite performance is not just about accumulating training hours—it's about precision, execution, and the ability to adapt in the face of competition challenges.

The Three Phases of Performance Development in THE SYSTEM™

Each athlete progresses through three distinct phases when applying THE SYSTEM™ to their training regimen:

1. Foundation Phase – Establishing the Base

Before achieving peak performance, athletes must build a strong aerobic base, refine their technique, and develop consistency. This phase focuses on:

- Endurance Training: Developing the aerobic engine with structured Zone 2 rides.

- Cadence Control: Refining pedaling efficiency and reducing wasted energy.

- Strength Development: Building force through low-cadence and tempo-based training.

● Mindset Training: Implementing effort control and resilience-building exercises.

2. Performance Phase – Building Strength and Speed

Once a solid base is established, athletes enter the performance phase, which focuses on enhancing power, increasing intensity, and optimizing race readiness. Key training elements include:

● VO2 Max & FRC Development: Structured intervals to boost sustained high-intensity efforts.

● Threshold & Lactate Clearance Work: Improving the ability to hold race pace for extended durations.

● Speed & Power Integration: Sprint-focused training to enhance explosive strength.

● Tactical Race Simulations: Practicing breakaways, surges, and race-day execution.

3. Peak Phase – Maximizing Performance on Race Day

The final phase ensures athletes reach their absolute peak at the right moment. This phase includes:

● Fine-tuning Energy System Efficiency: Refining pacing strategies to match race demands.

● Tapering for Peak Performance: Adjusting training volume and intensity to optimize freshness.

● Psychological Readiness: Race visualization and mental conditioning exercises.

● Final Pre-Race Workouts: Dialing in neuromuscular activation and priming the body for competition.

Real-World Application: Case Studies Using THE SYSTEM™

Case Study #1: Developing Aerobic Efficiency for Long-Distance Racing

● Athlete Profile: Endurance cyclist preparing for a 200-mile gravel race.

- THE SYSTEM™ Strategy: Emphasis on TTE and MFTP development with long-tempo efforts and sustained aerobic work.

- Results: Increased threshold power by 12% and improved fatigue resistance in the final 50 miles of racing.

Case Study #2: Boosting Sprint Power and Race-Day Speed

- Athlete Profile: Road racer needing more explosive power for finishing sprints.

- THE SYSTEM™ Strategy: Targeted Pmax and FRC training using sprint-specific workouts and over-speed drills.

- Results: 15% increase in peak power and improved finishing speed in criterium races.

Case Study #3: Mastering Energy Systems for Multi-Day Stage Racing

- Athlete Profile: Stage racer competing in a multi-day event with varied terrain.

- THE SYSTEM™ Strategy: Balanced VO2 Max, threshold, and stamina training to handle different race scenarios.

- Results: Improved ability to recover between stages, hold high power on climbs, and execute race tactics effectively.

Common Pitfalls and How THE SYSTEM™ Prevents Them

Even the most dedicated athletes can make mistakes in their training, often leading to plateaus, burnout, and inconsistent performance. Many athletes unknowingly sabotage their progress by focusing too much on one aspect of training while neglecting other critical components. THE SYSTEM™ provides a structured, data-driven approach that eliminates these pitfalls, ensuring sustainable performance gains.

Common Training Pitfalls and How THE SYSTEM™ Mitigates Them

✔ **Avoiding Overtraining:** Many athletes push too hard, leading to chronic fatigue and declining performance. THE SYSTEM™ incorporates structured recovery periods, effort control strategies, and biofeedback analysis to ensure optimal balance between intensity and recovery, preventing burnout.

✔ **Optimizing Training Load:** Too much or little training can hinder progress. THE SYSTEM™ utilizes data-driven adjustments and progressive overload principles to keep training loads appropriate, ensuring adaptation without excessive fatigue.

✔ **Balancing Energy Systems:** Focusing solely on endurance or high-intensity efforts can create weaknesses in performance. THE SYSTEM™ ensures comprehensive development across endurance, power, and speed, preventing gaps in fitness that could limit race-day performance.

✔ **Maintaining Mental Focus:** Inconsistent mental discipline can lead to poor execution during key moments in competition. THE SYSTEM™ integrates mental conditioning exercises, visualization techniques, and race-day strategies to reinforce focus, confidence, and resilience.

✔ **Eliminating Inefficiencies:** Poor cadence control, ineffective pacing, and unstructured workouts can reduce training effectiveness. THE SYSTEM™ emphasizes technique, execution, and real-time adjustments to enhance efficiency and maximize gains.

✔ **Sustaining Long-Term Progress:** Many athletes experience short bursts of improvement followed by stagnation. THE SYSTEM™ implements a structured, long-term progression model that keeps performance gains steady, sustainable, and measurable over time.

By addressing these common pitfalls, THE SYSTEM™ ensures that athletes train smarter, perform consistently, and achieve long-term success without unnecessary setbacks.

Final Thoughts: The Power of THE SYSTEM™ in Action

THE SYSTEM™ is not just about training hard—it's about training with purpose, precision, and intelligence. It is a methodology designed to bridge the gap between scientific principles and real-world application, ensuring that athletes optimize every facet of their performance. By embracing this structured approach, athletes gain a strategic edge, allowing them to peak at the right time and sustain high-level performance year after year.

Unlike conventional training plans that often focus on isolated elements, THE SYSTEM™ integrates all aspects of physical conditioning, mental resilience, energy system management, and tactical execution. This comprehensive framework empowers athletes to train smarter, race more effectively, and recover efficiently, leading to continuous progression and long-term success.

Athletes who fully commit to THE SYSTEM™ experience more than just improvements in power output or endurance—they develop a deeper understanding of their bodies, a refined ability to execute under pressure, and a mindset geared toward excellence.

This Approach Fosters:

✓ **Peak Performance on Demand:** Training cycles that align with key events ensure athletes reach their full potential when it matters most.

✓ **Sustainability and Longevity:** Intelligent workload management reduces burnout and keeps athletes progressing over seasons and years.

✓ **Strategic Race Execution:** Data-driven decision-making and refined tactics allow athletes to capitalize on strengths and mitigate weaknesses.

✓ **Mental and Emotional Mastery:** The integration of emotional intelligence and leadership skills builds confidence, focus, and resilience.

✓ **A Blueprint for Success:** Whether preparing for an endurance event, a criterium, or a multi-day stage race, THE SYSTEM™ provides the ultimate roadmap to reaching new heights.

At its core, THE SYSTEM™ is more than just a training framework—it's a movement toward intentional, informed, and transformative performance. The athletes who embrace it elevate not just their own capabilities but the very standard of what's possible in cycling and endurance sports.

The journey doesn't end here—it begins now. Commit to THE SYSTEM™ and unlock your highest level of performance.

Postface: The Journey Continues

The Commitment to Lifelong Mastery

Mastering peak performance is not a one-time event—it is an ongoing process of refinement, adaptation, and unwavering commitment. THE SYSTEM™ is not just a methodology; it is a way of thinking, training, and competing that evolves as you grow as an athlete. Whether you are striving for a personal best, preparing for your next race, or simply training to improve overall fitness, the journey never truly ends.

The Adaptability of THE SYSTEM™

The beauty of THE SYSTEM™ lies in its adaptability. No matter your level—whether you're just starting your journey or competing at an elite level—the framework remains the same:

✔ Train Smart – Prioritize structured, intentional workouts that align with your goals.

✔ Execute with Precision – Apply effort control, energy system optimization, and tactical race execution.

✔ Sustain Excellence – Develop mental resilience, leadership, and emotional intelligence to achieve long-term success.

Navigating the Ups and Downs of Progress

As you continue applying THE SYSTEM™, remember that progress is not always linear. Some days will feel like breakthroughs, while others may challenge your resolve. Setbacks are not failures—they are opportunities to refine, adapt, and grow.

✔ Stay Patient – Training adaptations take time. Trust in the process and avoid rushing progress.

✔ Stay Disciplined – Consistency over time will always outweigh short-term intensity.

✔ Stay Open to Learning – Each session provides insights. Keep evolving your approach.

✓ Stay Resilient – The greatest athletes are those who can embrace adversity and turn challenges into fuel for improvement.

Beyond Training: The Bigger Picture

The impact of THE SYSTEM™ extends beyond training logs and race results. It fosters a mindset of continuous growth, self-discipline, and perseverance that applies to every aspect of life. The lessons learned in training—patience, resilience, and adaptability—are the same qualities that lead to success in business, relationships, and personal development.

✓ You are not just an athlete—you are a lifelong learner.

✓ You are not just training for a race—you are training for excellence.

✓ You are not just following a plan—you are mastering a process.

The Journey Never Ends

Performance mastery is not a destination; it is a journey that extends as long as you remain committed to growth. The knowledge and strategies you have gained through THE SYSTEM™ will serve as your foundation, but true success comes from your commitment to continual evolution.

Wherever you are on this path, the next challenge is always ahead. Embrace it, own it, and continue pushing your limits—because the road to mastery never ends.

Book Series Summary

The System 6x6 Series: The Evolution of Execution Mastery

Here is a quick update on *The System 6x6* book series. Each volume continues to build upon the structured methodology, leading athletes from foundational training principles to peak execution mastery. Below is the finalized progression:

To fully understand the power of this movement, here's a breakdown of the four books in *The System 6x6* series:

- **Book 1 - The System 6x6 Framework** – Establishing the science and structure of training, this book lays the foundation for performance methodology, integrating physiological principles with structured development.

- **Book 2 - The System 6x6 Continuum** – Focused on the evolution of training and adaptation, this volume introduces an adaptive approach, ensuring long-term progress while preventing plateaus through strategic fatigue management.

- **Book 3 - The System 6x6 Execution Model** – Bridging the gap between training and performance, this book emphasizes effort control, tactical awareness, and decision-making under high-pressure conditions—transforming preparation into execution.

- **Book 4 - The System 6x6: Mastery in Motion** – The final evolution of performance mastery, turning structured training into instinctive, repeatable, high-level execution. This volume cements the *Good to Great* transformation, reinforcing sustained elite performance. Closing the gap between preparation and execution, ensuring that success is achieved and sustained.

- **Book 5 - The System 6x6: The 36th Chamber – Becoming The System**

Black Belt – Self-Mastery, Energy, and Presence

Taught Only by Coach David, Master Black Belt

The 36th Chamber is not a destination—it is a path.

An ongoing journey of presence, energy, and internal alignment.

It is the space where the teachings of The System stop being applied—and begin to live within you.

Created and taught exclusively by Coach David, the 36th Chamber is for those prepared to embody The System. It's a path of self-mastery that transcends metrics, goals, and even competition. Here, performance is no longer something you do—it is who you are.

From Human Doing to Human Being.

From Performer to Presence.

In martial arts, earning a black belt can take four to six years of disciplined study. But in truth, that achievement only marks the beginning of deeper learning. Likewise, stepping into the 36th Chamber initiates a lifetime of growth.

Inside are thirty-six living teachings—each one a chamber in its own right.

They cannot be conquered. They must be experienced.

Some will take months. Others, years. Some, a lifetime.

This is not a book to finish.

It is a way to live.

You no longer follow The System.

You become it.